Jim Elliot

Susan Martins Miller

Illustrated by
Ken Landgraf

BARBOUR
PUBLISHING, INC.
Uhrichsville, Ohio

Published by Barbour Publishing, Inc.
　　　　　　　P.O. Box 719
　　　　　　　Uhrichsville, Ohio 44683
　　　　　　　http://www.barbourbooks.com

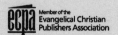 Member of the
Evangelical Christian
Publishers Association

Printed in the United States of America.

Jim
Elliot

GOD HAD PLANS FOR JIM ELLIOT.

1

Jim Elliot did not know where he was going. But he knew that he was going somewhere that God had planned for him.

He did not know when he would go. But he wanted to be ready when it was time to go.

Lots of students who start college do not know what kind of job they want to have when they finish going to school. They think they will have fun while they are in college, and then they can decide later what kind of job to get. But Jim was not like this. He knew what he wanted to do. He did not want an ordinary job in the United States. He was smart and could be anything he wanted to be—doctor, lawyer, pastor, or anything else. But he only wanted to be one thing. Someday, somewhere, he would be a missionary. Going to college was one way of getting ready for that occupation.

Such were Jim Elliot's thoughts when he started going to Wheaton College in 1945. But he had already started getting ready to be a missionary even when he was a little boy.

Jim grew up in the state of Oregon on the slope of a mountain called Mt. Tabor. His mother was a chiropractor and his father was a Bible teacher. His parents read the Bible to Jim and his brothers and sister every day, and every

THE ELLIOT FAMILY READ THE BIBLE DAILY.

day his father prayed with him. The whole family went to church every week. Jim's mother believed that it was good even for babies to learn to worship God.

Mr. and Mrs. Elliot believed in hard work, obedience, and honesty, and they tried to teach their children these qualities. The children had chores that they had to do every day. Jim's jobs included feeding chickens, stoking the furnace, cleaning up the yard, and running errands. His friends were surprised at how many chores he had to do, but Jim did not seem to mind. He just figured out the best way to get the work done and did the best he could. Sometimes he even got his friends to help him with his work. Because he grew up in such a family, Jim was not afraid of hard work, whether it was physical work or mental work.

But Jim knew how to have fun, too. He

JIM'S JOBS INCLUDED FEEDING THE CHICKENS.

liked to take two of his friends hunting and camping. The boys did not have any money for equipment, but that did not stop them. Jim looked in all the stores where they could buy used equipment until he found just what they needed. On their first hunting trip, they shot a duck. Unfortunately, it was someone's pet duck!

When he was in high school, Jim played on the football team and was in the school plays. Some of his teachers thought he had enough talent to be a professional actor. But Jim was not interested in that. He liked being in the plays while he was young, but being an actor was not as interesting as being a missionary would be.

Jim liked for people to know what he believed. He took his Bible with him to school and talked about what the Bible said with his

JIM WAS A TALENTED ACTOR.

friends. Many people who go to church are afraid to talk about God with their friends or to pray before they eat lunch if other people are watching. But not Jim. He made sure that people knew what he thought.

To go to Wheaton College, which is in Illinois, Jim had to move two thousand miles away from his family and all the things that he was used to. He did not have much money to pay for college, but this did not bother him. His parents had taught him that God would give him the things he needed. Even though he did not know where the money he needed would come from, Jim headed off to college to start getting ready for his future.

Jim was a very serious student. He was an adult now, and he wanted to make the best decisions he could. He was in college to prepare to be a missionary, so he did not want to waste

JIM ALWAYS PRAYED BEFORE MEALS.

valuable time doing things that had nothing to do with being a missionary. He spent his time studying for classes and reading the Bible and praying. He did not care about football games, basketball games, class picnics, or parties. While most of the other college students found time to do these things and have some fun, Jim thought it was a waste of time. He went to a football game once, just to see why everyone was so interested in it. He had played football in high school, so he knew all about the game. But he did not think college students and adults should be spending their time that way, especially not Christian students. When he heard all the cheering and shouting in the stands, he thought it was foolish to get so excited about something that was not very important. Wouldn't it be better if they used that energy for praising God instead of football players? He would rather stay in his

JIM THOUGHT FOOTBALL GAMES WERE A WASTE OF TIME.

room and pray while everyone else went to the game.

One decision that Jim made was to try out for the wrestling team. This was something new for him, but he thought he could do it. Jim had a good reason for trying to wrestle, and it was not because he thought it would be fun. Instead, he wrestled because it was a good way to stay healthy and build strength for the time in the future when he was a missionary. Many missionaries live in places where life is rugged and difficult. They have to be in good physical condition to live and work in a place like that. So Jim started wrestling in order to get in shape.

He turned out to be very good at wrestling, even though he had never tried it before. Once, when he was just learning to wrestle, Jim was in a match with a national wrestling champion.

JIM WRESTLED TO STAY PHYSICALLY FIT.

No one really expected that Jim would win. When the champion put a hold on Jim, everyone thought the match would soon be over. But he wriggled out of the champion's hold. So the champion put another hold on him. And another one after that. Jim surprised everyone by squirming out of hold after hold. Before long, the champion was embarrassed and frustrated, and he was never able to pin down Jim Elliot. That was the day the rest of the team discovered that Jim was double-jointed and could bend his body in ways that most people couldn't. After that, they called him Rubberneck Elliot.

It must have been fun to frustrate a national champion the way Jim did. But to Jim, it did not matter if he won or lost the wrestling match, as long as he stayed physically fit.

Jim was very careful about the way he ate, too. In the cafeteria line, he chose his food on

JIM WAS NICKNAMED "RUBBERNECK ELLIOT."

the basis of how food could help him be a better missionary. He stayed away from junk food and desserts. Instead, he ate lots of fruit, vegetables, and grains—foods that would help his body stay healthy. He had to be strong and well for the harsh missionary life he wanted.

At the end of his first year of college, Jim was satisfied with what he had accomplished. He had done well in his classes, and that was important. But it was even more important that he had gotten closer to God during that year. He could see that he was making progress toward his goal of becoming a missionary. He had learned a lot, both academically and spiritually. And, he had kept himself in good shape physically.

Jim ended the year the way he had started it—with very little money. After being away from home for nine months, he wanted to see

HE ATE LOTS OF FRUIT, VEGETABLES AND GRAINS.

his family. But he could not afford to take a bus or a train. So he hitchhiked. It took him only three days to go two thousand miles. He never waited more than fifteen minutes for a ride, and he got home to Oregon with $1.32 extra in his pocket. To Jim, this was proof that God was taking care of his needs. And this was the God he wanted to serve with his life.

IT TOOK HIM THREE DAYS TO GO TWO THOUSAND MILES.

"GLORY, BROTHER, WHAT'S YOUR VERSE FOR TODAY?"

2

"Glory, brother, what's your verse for today?"

This was Jim Elliot's way of saying good morning when he sat down to breakfast with his classmates. Before breakfast every day, Jim always took time for studying the Bible and praying. This was a very important habit for him. Often he found a verse that he liked especially well, one that he thought would help him during the day. That was his "verse for the day."

Jim believed everyone should start the day with reading the Bible and praying. It was such a beneficial habit; why wouldn't everyone do it? So it was natural for him to think that everyone had a verse for the day. Sometimes Jim embarrassed his classmates because they did not have an answer to his question, and they did not want to admit that they had not read the Bible that day. Some of the students even avoided sitting with Jim for a meal because they did not want him to ask them for a verse.

Jim Elliot was handsome, smart, and friendly. He could have been friends with anyone at the college. In fact, at the end of four years of college, he was very popular. Jim was friendly to everyone, but he was careful about how he chose his best friends.

One of the students who wrestled with Jim

SOME OF THE STUDENTS AVOIDED SITTING WITH JIM.

on the Wheaton College team was David Howard. During his first year of college, when he did not get to know many other people, Jim became good friends with Dave. At first, wrestling brought them together. They soon discovered that they had many things in common, especially an interest in becoming a missionary after college. This gave them reasons to do things together other than wrestling. Eventually, Jim and Dave decided to live across the hall from each other in the same dormitory so they could be together as much as they wanted.

Jim and Dave were both involved with a group of college students who were also interested in becoming missionaries. Most of the people that Jim knew best were in this group. They had meetings to learn about becoming missionaries to other countries.

Sometimes these students traveled around

JIM TOOK PART IN A MISSIONS GROUP.

to nearby cities and states. They gave talks to groups in churches and schools and explained to other people that many places in the world had no missionaries. The people in those countries did not know that God had made them and loved them and had sent His son, Jesus, to show the way to God. Jim would get up in front of a room full of strangers, people he had never met before and would probably never see again, and challenge them to think about missionary work. He spoke so convincingly because he really believed what he was saying. Many, many missionaries were needed to go all over the world and tell this good news.

Jim wanted to go to another country and even to a place far away from any cities. He even thought about going to a place where no missionaries had gone before. The more Jim learned about missionary work, the more he

JIM WOULD SPEAK TO A ROOM FULL OF STRANGERS.

wanted to do this. As he talked to other people, he challenged them to see that they could become missionaries themselves, or they could pray and give money to people who wanted to be missionaries.

Jim concentrated so much on preparing to be a missionary that he was not interested in having a girlfriend while he was in college. He did not go to parties and games and events where men and women students could get to know each other. Many of the girls wanted to go on a date with him, but Jim was not interested. In fact, he stayed away from them on purpose. He thought he could be a better missionary if he did not get married. If he got married, he might be distracted from serving God with his whole heart. The responsibility of a wife and children would be a serious commitment that might take him away from important

MANY GIRLS WANTED TO DATE JIM.

work. Besides, he wanted to be a missionary in places where it would be difficult to live; it would not be fair to ask a wife to go to a place like that. So Jim did not go out on dates, and he did not think anyone who was serious about being a missionary should. For instance, his friend Dave Howard went out on dates. When Dave came back to the dormitory after an evening out, Jim would say something like, "Have you been out with Phyllis again?" Obviously, he did not approve. In his opinion, Dave was wasting valuable time that he could have spent reading his Bible and praying. How was going on a date going to help him be a better missionary?

David Howard had a sister, Elisabeth, who also attended Wheaton College. She was one year older than Jim and Dave. She was also very interested in becoming a missionary, probably in Africa. Although Jim and Elisabeth had

"HAVE YOU BEEN OUT WITH PHYLLIS AGAIN?"

a lot in common, they did not meet until Elisabeth was almost finished with college.

When he met Elisabeth, Jim's world turned upside down. He was not looking for a girl-friend or a wife, but there she was. At first they just saw each other in class. They were both studying Greek so that they could learn to translate the Bible into other languages. During Elisabeth's last semester of college, Jim was in almost all of her classes. Then they started working on their homework together in the library. He had never met a woman like Elisabeth before. She was extremely intelligent —Jim thought maybe she was even smarter than he was. She probed the Bible as deeply as he did, and she had the same intense commit-ment to serve God that he had, and he admired the way she was trying to do what God wanted her to do, even leaving her family and going to

THEY STARTED WORKING ON HOMEWORK TOGETHER.

Africa. It did not take Jim long to see that if he was ever going to get married, he would want to marry Elisabeth. He debated what to do and finally decided to tell her the truth about how he felt. Just before she graduated from college and left Wheaton, they went on a picnic with other students planning to be missionaries. Afterwards, they stayed behind to clean up and walk back to campus together. Jim told Elisabeth that he loved her, and he could tell that she felt the same way.

But he still did not think that God wanted him to get married. He believed he should be a missionary as a single man. On the one hand, he loved Elisabeth. On the other hand, he did not think he would ever get married. It was hard to figure out why God let him love Elisabeth if He did not want him to get married. But Jim would not do anything that he was not

JIM AND ELISABETH WENT ON A PICNIC.

absolutely sure God wanted him to do. And
he still believed God wanted him to be a single
missionary. Besides, Elisabeth thought God
wanted her to go to Africa, and Jim thought
God wanted him to go to Latin America. A
whole ocean was going to separate them the
rest of their lives if they both obeyed God. They
could not even think about getting married.

One other student was a special friend of
Jim's. His name was Ed McCully. Ed was a
leader at the college, class president, an out-
standing athlete, and a championship speaker.
He even won a national award for a speech he
gave. Everyone at the college was impressed by
this achievement—everyone except Jim Elliot.

One day, after Ed had won the award, Jim
ran into him in the locker room at Wheaton
College after a workout. Jim grabbed Ed by the
neck and said, "Hey, McCully, so you won the

JIM SAW ED IN THE LOCKER ROOM.

national contest. Great stuff, McCully. You have a lot of talent, don't you? Where'd you get that ability? You know where you got it. God gave it to you. So what are you going to do with it? Spend it on yourself making money for yourself? You have no business doing that. You ought to be a missionary. I'm praying that God will make you one."

Now Ed was planning to be a lawyer, not a missionary. And everyone agreed he would be a great lawyer. But Jim did not let that stop him. He told Ed McCully exactly what he thought.

He did not change Ed's mind, though. Ed went on to law school the next year, while Jim continued his journey toward being a missionary.

"YOU OUGHT TO BE A MISSIONARY."

WHAT TO DO AFTER GRADUATION?

3

When Jim Elliot graduated from Wheaton College, he had no idea what he was going to do next. Most people who finish college try to get a good job and live on their own as adults. Jim's parents and other friends thought he should be a Bible teacher; he had studied the Bible so much over the years that he had become very good at teaching from the Bible. Or he could be a speaker who could talk about missions. If he traveled around the country, they thought, talking to college students, he could convince many people to become missionaries. Maybe these things were even more important than being a missionary himself.

Jim's older brother was already a missionary in Latin America, so Jim could understand that it would be hard for his parents to send another son off to a faraway and dangerous place. But he was determined to go. Too many people in other countries needed to know about God's love. He just could not stay in the United States and live a comfortable life knowing that all those people in other countries did not know God.

The problem was that Jim still did not know where he would go—or when. He was waiting for God to tell him the time and the place. So

HE WAS WAITING FOR GOD TO TELL HIM.

instead of starting a career after he finished college, Jim moved back to Oregon to live with his parents. He did odd jobs around his church and home, and he spent many hours a day reading stories about other missionaries, studying his Bible, and praying. After a while, he got a job as a substitute teacher in a high school. Some people thought Jim was being lazy and not even trying to get a real job. But Jim knew that what he was doing was important. Even in these small ways, God was getting Jim ready for what would happen in the future.

About one year after he finished college, Jim attended some special language training in Oklahoma. He spent most of the summer of 1950 learning how to listen to a language that he did not know and writing down the sounds that he heard. Then he would look for patterns in the sounds and form words and sentences.

EARTH

HE GOT A JOB AS A SUBSTITUTE TEACHER.

Many languages around the world do not have alphabets that people can write down; the people do not learn to read because their language is never written down. Jim wanted to learn to write down one of these languages so that he could translate the Bible into it. He would learn the language, write it down, and teach people to read their own language. Then they could read the Bible themselves.

The class used missionaries who had already learned a language this way to help the students practice their skills. Jim's helper was a man who had lived in Ecuador and worked with a language called Quichua. There were thousands and thousands of Quichua Indians in Ecuador and very few missionaries. For a long time, Jim had been interested in going to South America. Now he started wondering if he should go to Ecuador. He decided that for ten

JIM'S HELPER WAS A MAN WHO LIVED IN ECUADOR.

days, he would pray three times a day asking God whether he should go to Ecuador. He had a friend, Bill Cathers, who was also thinking about the same thing, and it was exciting to think that they might be able to go to Ecuador as a team and live among the Quichuas. Going with another man as his partner was exactly what Jim wanted to do.

Something else interested Jim. Near the Quichua area in Ecuador was another tribe, the Aucas. While the Quichuas numbered in the thousands, there were only a few hundred Aucas. The Quichuas had a few missionaries, but the Aucas had none. No one outside their own tribe had ever been able to get close to the Aucas. Some missionaries had learned the Quichua language, but no one had ever been able to get close enough to the Aucas to learn their language. In fact, the Aucas were a violent

THE AUCA TRIBE LIVED NEAR THE QUICHUAS.

tribe. They had killed many people who had crossed into their territory. Sometimes they killed people for no reason at all—including people in their own tribe. Even the Quichuas did not feel safe if the Aucas were nearby. It seemed impossible that missionaries could ever reach them.

But reaching such people was exactly what Jim wanted to do. For years, ever since he was a boy, he had been getting ready for the day when God asked him to do something like this—to live in a remote place and reach a group of people with the news of God's love.

After ten days of prayer, Jim decided that God did want him to go to Ecuador. He soon wrote to his parents to tell them of this decision. Jim and his friend, Bill Cathers, decided to stay in Oklahoma for a few more weeks while they sorted out everything they needed to

HE SOON TOLD HIS PARENTS OF HIS DECISION.

do to get ready to go to Ecuador. Jim was convinced that he had done the right thing in not getting married—although his feelings for Elisabeth Howard were very strong. Two single men working together was the best kind of team for missionary work.

But things did not work out quite the way Jim hoped. Bill Cathers decided to get married. He still wanted to go to Ecuador, but he would get married first, and he probably would not go to the remote and isolated kind of place that Jim had in mind.

Jim was still convinced that two men working together was the best way to go. But since Bill was getting married, he had to find another partner. That's when he heard that his old friend from college, Ed McCully, had decided to drop out of law school and become a missionary. More than a year had passed since Jim

ED MCCULLY HAD BECOME A MISSIONARY.

had told Ed that he was praying that God would make him a missionary, but finally his prayers had been answered. Instead of going home to Oregon, Jim traveled to Milwaukee, Wisconsin, to be with Ed and talk about their future.

Ed and Jim decided that they should spend a few months in ministry together in the United States. They went to a small town, Chester, Illinois, and started a Sunday school, visited prisoners, spoke in schools, and produced a radio program. They got along well together and had many of the same goals. It seemed as if they would be a good match for going to Ecuador together. Jim applied for a passport so he would be ready to leave the United States.

Then Ed McCully decided to get married. First Bill, now Ed. Jim was the only one who still believed that being single was the best

THEY VISITED PRISONERS.

thing for a missionary in a primitive place. Like Bill, Ed and his wife still planned to go to Ecuador, and they still wanted to work with Jim. But they were going to take a year of basic medical training first.

So Jim had to start looking for a partner all over again. This time he went back home to Portland to wait for the next step. While he was in Portland, a missionary from Ecuador visited his family. Dr. Tidmarsh had been a missionary among the Quichua Indians, and he and Jim had been writing letters to each other. Because his wife was ill, Dr. Tidmarsh had to leave the work with the Quichuas. He hoped that Jim could come and take over.

Meeting Dr. Tidmarsh in person made Jim even more determined to go to Ecuador—as soon as he could find a partner. He decided to visit a friend in Seattle, Pete Fleming. The

DR. TIDMARSH HAD BEEN A MISSIONARY TO THE QUICHUAS.

Fleming and the Elliot families had known each other for many years. Pete was studying to be a teacher, but he had recently decided that perhaps God wanted him to be a missionary. He was not sure he could really do much good in the world as a teacher, but he could as a missionary. So when Jim Elliot came along and suggested the idea that they should go to Ecuador together, Pete was ready. Although Pete had a girlfriend and was very close to getting married, too, he decided he should stay single, at least for a while, and go to Ecuador with Jim. Pete made his decision very quickly, and from then on, he and Jim made serious plans to sail for Ecuador in just a few months.

PETE AND JIM MADE THEIR PLANS.

HEAT AND HUMIDITY BLASTED THEM IN ECUADOR.

4

Heat and humidity blasted them in the face on the day that Jim Elliot and Pete Fleming landed in Ecuador. It was February 21, 1952. They had been at sea for eighteen days, and they were excited and anxious to finally be in Ecuador. The port at Guayaquil, Ecuador, was a welcome sight.

They got off the ship and tried to absorb

their surroundings—a sea of faces in all directions, store windows displaying a wide variety of goods from sweaters and typewriters to fake shrunken Indian heads. To everyone around them, it was an ordinary day. For Jim and Pete, it was like no other day they had ever lived. The day was the beginning of a future with many questions and challenges.

The first challenge was to figure out where they were supposed to go after getting off the ship. Jim had been sending letters to Dr. Tidmarsh, and they thought he would meet them when the ship came into port. He examined the faces of everyone in the crowd, but he could not spot Dr. Tidmarsh. He was nowhere around, and Jim did not know how to contact him. He and Pete were going to have to do the best they could on their own in a strange place where people did not speak their language.

STORE WINDOWS DISPLAYED A VARIETY OF GOODS.

Using the little bit of Spanish that Jim knew, they found their way to a run-down hotel and tried to get some sleep. But they could not sleep very much. The room was infested with mosquitos, and it was not long before the two young men were covered with bites. They tossed and turned in the unbearable heat. Jim heard the town clock ring every fifteen minutes all night—along with a braying burro and a dance band. Three days later, he was still scratching from the mosquito bites. This was not exactly the grand beginning to missionary life that he had imagined.

The next morning, things got better. Dr. Tidmarsh arrived, and they had a long talk about the work ahead of them. Dr. Tidmarsh would get Jim and Pete started at Shandia, the mission station where he had been working for many years. Once they were used to the work,

THE ROOM WAS FULL OF MOSQUITOES.

he would leave and they would be on their own. He could visit them for a few days at a time, but his wife's health would not allow them to live in the jungle anymore.

The three of them started their journey by flying to Quito, the capital of Ecuador. Quito was a very old city, set between two mountain ranges. On one side was a smoking volcano. All kinds of people lived in the city—from beggars in rags to rich people in expensive clothes, people pounding cocoa beans with their feet, a boy with a monkey on his head.

As interesting as the city was, Jim had not come there to be a tourist. Quito was a stepping stone for Jim and Pete. While they were there, their main job was to learn Spanish so that they could go out on their own. Once they learned Spanish, they could move to Shandia. They found a teacher and gathered their books

ALL KINDS OF PEOPLE LIVED IN THE CITY.

and started to study.

At first, their progress was slow. It was too easy to slip into English because they were with other missionaries a lot of the time. It was natural to speak English. What they needed was to be surrounded by Spanish-speaking people, to be with people who did not speak any English at all. After about two months, they found a room to rent with an Ecuadorian doctor and his family. This plunged them into Spanish all the time, forcing them to speak Spanish and expand their vocabulary. The five children in the house were delighted to correct the mistakes Jim and Pete made. Now their rate of progress was better. They were determined to learn Spanish quickly so they could move on to Quichua territory—one step closer to the Aucas.

One problem made it difficult for Jim to concentrate at times. Although he had not seen

THE CHILDREN HELPED JIM LEARN.

Elisabeth Howard for a long time, he still thought of her frequently; and they had been writing letters back and forth. She had not been able to go to Africa after all. Even though she had been dreaming of Africa for a long time, Elisabeth had decided that God did not want her to go there. Instead, he wanted her to go to Ecuador. So a few weeks after Jim's arrival, Elisabeth arrived in Ecuador, too.

Now Jim wondered if he should ask Elisabeth to marry him. They had both come to Ecuador because they wanted to obey God, not just so they could be together. Perhaps God meant for them to be life partners. But Jim was not ready to get engaged. He still believed that he could be a better missionary to a primitive tribe if he stayed single. It could be years before he could get married. He made no promises to Elisabeth.

SOON ELISABETH ARRIVED IN ECUADOR, TOO.

Even though Jim and Elisabeth did not make plans to get married, they enjoyed being together. Elisabeth and her missionary partner found a room with a family just across the street from where Jim and Pete were living. The four of them threw themselves into language study as their first priority. The sooner they learned Spanish, the sooner they could move on to jungle work. They studied long and hard hours.

Jim and Elisabeth found time to relax together, too. They took long walks exploring every corner of Quito, seeing the outdoor markets, museums, and craft shops. Once, with a group of friends, they got up at 2:00 in the morning to climb a mountain and watch the sun rise. For the first time since Elisabeth graduated from college, they could see each other every day and talk as much as they wanted to.

THEY TOOK LONG WALKS EXPLORING QUITO.

After Jim had been in Ecuador about four months, he had the chance to fly in a plane over the jungle of eastern Ecuador. This is where he eventually wanted to live and work. The plane ride was his first chance to look for some evidence of where the mysterious Auca tribe might be. Since they were not a very big tribe, the Aucas could remain hidden deep in the jungle, and for months at a time no outsiders would see them.

Jim and the other missionaries had heard that the Quichua Indians, a much gentler tribe, in the eastern jungle had had some friendly contact with the Aucas. Normally, the Aucas were known for their brutal treatment of anyone outside their tribe, even other Indian groups. So the possibility that Quichuas were getting along with Aucas was encouraging. But it turned out not to be true. In fact, the truth was

HE FLEW IN A PLANE OVER THE JUNGLE.

that the Aucas had recently killed five Quichuas in that area.

Jim did not spot the Aucas on that trip. But
he determined that someday he would find
them. Compared to the millions of people in
Ecuador and all of South America, the Aucas
were a small group and not very important. But
to Jim they were important. They knew nothing
about the love of God, and he wanted to reach
them with this good news. He went back to
Quito more determined than ever.

When August came, five months after he
arrived in Quito, Jim was ready to move on. His
Spanish was very good; some people who heard
him talk could not believe that he had only been
in Ecuador for five short months. His hard work
had paid off.

Elisabeth did not yet know where she would
be working. First she had to finish her language

HE RETURNED MORE DETERMINED THAN EVER.

study. With excitement and reluctance, Jim said good-bye to Elisabeth and, with Pete, headed for the jungles.

JIM AND PETE HEADED FOR THE JUNGLES.

A GOOD KNIFE WAS ESSENTIAL.

5

Jim Elliot had never needed a machete before. Now he needed one every day. In Shandia, a good sharp knife was essential to daily activities.

There were no roads going to Shandia, so Jim and Pete went by air. Only there was no place to land a plane at Shandia, so they had to be dropped off at the nearest little town that had an airstrip, Pano. From there, they hiked through the jungle to Shandia, with a guide using a machete to cut a clean path. The ground was slippery. Sometimes they were up to their knees in mud. They hiked like this for hours, trying to reach Shandia before darkness fell. In the dark, even the guides might not find their way out of the jungle. Just as the moon appeared in the sky, they reached the clearing that was their new home. The Indians gathered around them, curious about the new missionaries. Jim and Pete were relieved to see Dr. Tidmarsh's bamboo home ready and waiting for them.

The next day they had to go back to Pano for more of their tools and supplies. They did this again and again until they had everything they needed to start working. Without an airstrip, this was the only way to get the things they needed.

THE INDIANS GATHERED AROUND THEM.

Shandia was high on a cliff above the Atun Yaku River. Nearby were the Shandia River and the Napo River. Even though it was a primitive place—without running water or electricity or roads—Jim thought Shandia was beautiful. The bird songs in the forest enchanted him with their long, low whistles, canarylike tunes or mellow hoots. At night, he heard the racket of crickets and other insects. The sounds were so fantastic that Jim thought he might record the night sounds for others to hear, from the squeaking bats in the thatched roof to the thundering rapids of the river below the cliff.

Jim and Pete had three main jobs that they needed to do at Shandia. First, they had to learn the Quichua language. When they studied Spanish in Quito, they had a teacher and written textbooks to help them learn. But Quichua was a language that was not written down. They

THE BIRD SONGS ENCHANTED HIM.

had to learn just by listening to the Indians talk and trying to identify the sounds and words. They carried little notebooks everywhere they went and wrote everything down so they could study their notes more carefully later. Jim's linguistic training from two years earlier was coming in handy now.

Their second job was to build some buildings—houses for missionaries who would join them later, and a school, and a clinic. They hoped that someday Shandia would be an active, thriving center for missionary work. Jim's experience doing odd jobs while living with his parents in Portland was important now. He knew a lot about carpentry.

The third task was to clear a strip of land and make a place where an airplane could land. With their own airstrip, they would be able to get supplies more quickly and without having

THEIR SECOND JOB WAS TO BUILD SHELTERS.

to make the long, muddy hike to Pano. Jim hired about forty Quichua men to work on clearing the airstrip. He would get them going on the work, and then he and Pete would spend their time in the house studying language. They lived in a simple structure, with boards for the floor and bamboo walls and ceiling. They could look out the windows to see the river, the air-strip, the garden, and even thick forest only a few feet away. It was a nice place to study. The more time they spent on language study, the sooner they would be able to communicate with the Quichuas.

Finding time to study was not as easy as it sounds, though. They were constantly interrupted because the Indians needed help. Neither Jim nor Pete had any medical training, but they had to learn quickly about ways to help the illnesses and injuries of the jungle. Dr.

QUICHUA MEN CLEARED AN AIR STRIP.

Tidmarsh was a doctor of philosophy and not a medical doctor. But he had years of experience in jungle work and had learned a lot about medicine over the years. Jim and Pete tried to learn as much as they could from him before he left them on their own.

They had a limited supply of drugs, but they learned to use the ones they had properly. Sometimes it would be a sick baby that they took care of. One time, they loaned kerosene to a family so they could keep their lamp going all night while they sat up with the baby. Instead, everyone in the house went to sleep, and the baby died.

Another time, a twelve-year-old girl had been bitten by a snake. When he heard the screaming, Jim scrambled to do what he could; he knew he had to get the poison out of the girl's body before it killed her. He stuck a clean

THEY TOOK CARE OF SICK CHILDREN.

blade on his scalpel and slit her skin to release the venom. But the girl's cries of pain made her family think Jim was hurting her, and they made him stop. Then he tried to suck the snake's venom out of the girl, but she screamed again. It was frustrating to know the best thing to do and not be allowed to do it.

The Quichuas were very superstitious people. If the missionaries could not help them, the Quichuas would call in the witch doctor. He would perform rituals and traditional cures, but really, he was powerless. He could not keep people from getting sick and dying. When this happened, Jim and Pete faced their greatest challenge. Even if they knew what to do, the superstitions of the Quichuas might hold them back, and they would not be allowed to help. What was considered a minor illness in the United States could threaten to kill a child in

THE WITCH DOCTOR COULD NOT HELP PEOPLE.

the jungle, and it was not long before Jim realized that death was a way of life in the jungle. He wrote to his parents on the day that he built his first coffin for a baby born dead, knowing that he would probably have to make many more.

The superstitious way of life among the Quichuas made Jim and Pete work even harder at their language study. If they could teach the Quichuas the truth about God and His power, the Quichuas could be freed from the superstition that ruled their lives. Jim was convinced that the Quichuas needed to learn to read the Bible for themselves so that they could teach their own people. He was determined to open the school that Dr. Tidmarsh had to close.

The airstrip was finished on September 30, 1952, only a few weeks after their arrival at

HE BUILT HIS FIRST COFFIN FOR A BABY.

Shandia. More than 150 Indians gathered to watch as the Piper landed with its load of bread, meat, vegetables, sugar, and lentils. Elisabeth, who was working on the other side of the country, had known that the plane was going, and she made sure there was something special on it for Jim—honey, peanut butter, candy, and crackers. Now at least they could get the supplies they needed to keep working and food and medicine to stay healthy.

For years, Jim had concentrated on making himself ready for rugged missionary work. He had worked to be in good shape physically and to be close to God spiritually. At last, those years of focusing on the future goal were paying off. Even so, Jim sometimes got discouraged. He had mastered Spanish in only five months. But after three months at Shandia, he still knew almost no Quichua. He had memorized a few

MANY INDIANS WATCHED THE PLANE LAND.

practical phrases, but he could not carry on a conversation with his neighbors, much less preach a sermon or teach a Bible lesson. In Quito, his main task was to learn Spanish. But in Shandia, he had little time to learn the language. So many other things took up his time. He could not very well tell the parents of a sick baby that he did not have time to help them because he was too busy studying.

When they had been in the jungle for less than six months, Pete Fleming got sick with malaria and had to fly to Quito for several weeks until he got well. Pete's illness left Jim on his own in Shandia, and now the work went even slower. He felt like he was running from one crisis to another all day long. But he kept at it.

Jim and Pete were carving a place for themselves in the jungle. They learned to swing a

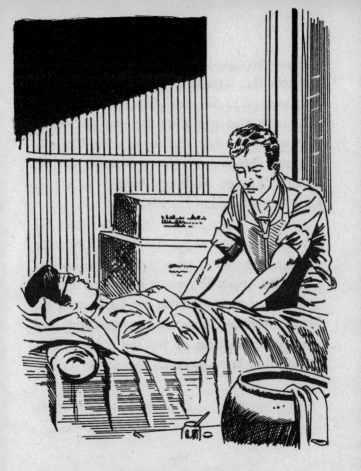

PETE FLEMING CONTRACTED MALARIA.

machete through the thick vegetation and to eat the foods that were available around them. Jim even learned to eat ants! The young missionaries were also preparing the way for others who would join them. Ed and Marilou McCully were still planning to come to Shandia as soon as they finished studying Spanish in Quito. Then they would have a solid team.

Jim was eager for the future to come. He had not forgotten about the Aucas. Once the work in Shandia was more stable, he still hoped to find the Aucas. Whenever he looked into the jungle, he remembered that the Aucas were out there somewhere. He wanted to find them. And when he found them, he was not going to give up until they knew the truth about God.

JIM EVEN LEARNED TO EAT ANTS.

ECUADOR'S RAINY SEASON IS DIFFICULT.

6

The rainy season in the jungles of Ecuador is not something to take lightly. Once the rains begin, people living in the jungle must adjust their activities and wait for the season to end.

In 1953, the rainy season was especially bad—perhaps the worst in thirty years. The projects that Jim Elliot and Pete Fleming had been working on for almost a year came to a stop. It was almost impossible to keep working on construction projects in the rain and mud. Jim and Pete had to stay indoors; all they could do was stand at the window and watch the water come down in thick sheets. Puddles formed in the clearing; then the puddles overflowed with oozing mud. The ground could not absorb another drop of moisture.

Within a few weeks, the weather turned dangerous. The river below the Shandia mission station rose to very high levels, and the cliff above it began to crumble. All the work that Pete and Jim had done for the last year was too close to the water. If the cliff fell, the buildings would fall into the rushing currents. They had no choice but to move the buildings. Even though the rain continued and the mud was knee-deep, they got their crew together and started taking apart the house that they had built

THEY TOOK DOWN THE HOUSE.

for Ed and Marilou McCully, who were supposed to arrive in a few months. They rebuilt the house farther from the river.

But the rains kept coming. At the end of July, it rained for four days straight. On the fifth day, they knew there was no escape from the damage the rains would do.

Jim and Pete forced themselves to work on the Quichua dictionary in the morning, despite their worries about the weather. About noon, they looked out and saw that the cliff had begun to break off. Water was surging toward them. They were going to lose their own house within a matter of hours.

Frantically, they packed their equipment and, with the help of a few of the Quichuas, started hauling it to the edge of the jungle, away from the water. In the few hours that they had, they took down the walls, the floor, the window

FRANTICALLY, THEY PACKED THEIR EQUIPMENT.

screens—everything they could. These supplies were too valuable to abandon to the raging river. Boxes of food, clothes, papers, and medical supplies were hauled away from the crumbling cliff. While Jim finished up at the house, Pete started on the medical clinic. This was the newest and best of their buildings. Having to tear it down was heart-wrenching, but they had no choice. Pete pulled out cupboards, doors, floor timbers, whatever they could pry loose.

They ran out of time. Jim was pulling out window screens from the house when the front porch gave way and dropped into the river. Jim scrambled to get to higher ground. Within only a few minutes, what was left of the house pitched over the cliff. Jim and Pete watched it go, helpless to stop the heaving force that snatched away in a few moments

THE HOUSE PITCHED OVER THE CLIFF.

what had taken them a year to do.

Still the rains came. They kept moving supplies from the buildings that stood closer to the edge of the jungle. Jim lost his shoes in the mud. Now his feet were scratched and cut with every step he took. But he could not stop for his own comfort. For six long, wet, dark hours, they lugged their equipment into the jungle. They lurched through the mud with staggering loads, not knowing how many trips they would be able to make before the river caught up with them.

Chunks of land and trees gave way to the thunderous power of the river. Jim and Pete hardly dared to look behind them to see what they were losing.

Exhausted and having done all they could at three o'clock in the morning, Pete and Jim huddled in some blankets at the home of one of

THEY LUGGED EQUIPMENT TO THE JUNGLE.

the Quichuas and tried to sleep. After only a couple of hours, one of the Quichuas came running to wake them, shouting about the water. They raced back to the mission station to see that the edge of the water was now only thirty feet from where they had left all their equipment. They would have to move everything again! They cut a trail deeper into the jungle.

By the middle of the morning, the river seemed to level out, and they thought that they were out of danger at last. But so much damage had been done! The McCully's house, which they already had moved once, was now a few feet from the edge of the broken cliff. Five other buildings, the playing field, and a part of the airstrip were completely gone. A year's worth of work had disappeared.

At her own mission station only a few miles away, Elisabeth Howard was standing by

THEY CUT A TRAIL DEEPER INTO THE JUNGLE.

her radio, anxious for news about what was happening at Shandia. She had talked to Jim on the radio two days earlier and knew that the weather was deteriorating and becoming dangerous. After two days of silence, she was worried about what had happened. She tried to find a messenger who would go to find out, but the runners refused to make the trip; it was too hazardous. Finally, she found someone who would go.

Jim sent back a letter that said, "Shandia is no more." Jim and Pete planned to set up a tent for temporary shelter while they sorted out what was left of their mission station. It seemed almost hopeless to think of going on.

When she received Jim's letter, Elisabeth left immediately for Shandia with a group of Indians. Pete and Jim would need all the help they could get.

ELISABETH WAS WORRIED ABOUT WHAT HAD HAPPENED.

When the rains let up and it was safe to be on the river, the missionaries had to decide what to do next. Jim and Pete, along with Ed McCully spent three weeks hiking through the jungle and paddling a canoe on the river to survey the area around Shandia. They visited Quichua villages, estimated how many Quichuas there were and tried to decide on a new place to build a mission station.

The best spot seemed to be a place called Puyupungu. One of the Quichua Indians who had fifteen children had begged them to come and start a school there. If they tried to go to a village where they had not been invited, it would be very difficult to open a station. But in Puyupungu they would be welcome guests.

Then the question became, who should go to Puyupungu? Ed and Marilou McCully were still studying Spanish and had not yet begun

THEY PADDLED A CANOE ON THE RIVER.

to learn Quichua. They could not start a new mission station from scratch and have any time to learn Quichua. It made more sense for Ed and Marilou to go to Shandia and live in a simple house while they rebuilt that station and studied Quichua. If Pete stayed at Shandia with them, he could help with construction and language study.

That left Jim to go to Puyupungu. But everyone thought it would be best if a married couple worked together to start the school and open a mission station. Jim and Elisabeth had often talked about getting married. They had even gotten engaged, although they had not decided when they would get married. Suddenly, the time was right.

In October of 1953, three months after the flood destroyed Shandia, Jim Elliot and Elisabeth Howard got married. There was no fancy

JIM LEFT TO GO TO PUYUPUNGO.

church wedding or satin bridal gown, no guests, no elaborate reception. They got married in a simple ceremony with the McCullys as witnesses. They signed their names in the huge legal register and were declared to be husband and wife.

THEY BECAME HUSBAND AND WIFE.

THEY STUDIED A MAP OF EASTERN ECUADOR.

7

They were on their knees, but they were not praying. They raised their hands and gestured, but it was not in praise.

Instead, Nate Saint, Ed McCully, and Jim Elliot were on the floor of Nate's house, studying a map of the jungles of eastern Ecuador. It was October of 1955, and they had decided that it was time to begin a serious search for the

Auca tribe. They knew they were all living on the edge of Auca territory, yet they could not point to a place on the map and say that's where the Aucas are. But they thought they were getting close.

Even though they did not know exactly where the Aucas were, the missionaries knew a lot about the tribe. They knew the Aucas were known for being brutal and murdering people for no reason. Not only did Aucas kill outsiders who came into their territory, but they also killed each other. Sometimes two families in the tribe would have an argument and attack each other. Sometimes a whole family would be killed because of an argument.

The Aucas taught their little boys to throw spears accurately and swiftly. For a target they used a figure of a human being; the boys would throw spear after spear until they knew that they

AUCA BOYS LEARNED TO THROW SPEARS.

could kill someone if they wanted to.

Some people thought that the Aucas might someday respond to friendship from outsiders. Most people thought that they would just keep on killing anyone who came near them. The missionaries wanted to try to reach them. Jim Elliot learned everything he could about them. He even found a woman, Dayuma, who had left the tribe when she was a girl and who had come to live among the peaceful Quichuas. Dayuma helped Jim to learn some Auca words and phrases. He wrote them down on note cards and carried them with him all the time so he could study them whenever he had a few moments. He learned to say "I like you." "I want to be your friend." "I want to approach you." "What is your name?" He practiced them over and over again, getting ready for the day when he would speak them to the Aucas.

DAYUMA HELPED JIM LEARN AUCA WORDS.

Nate Saint, the pilot, kept looking for the Aucas from the air. When Nate finally spotted a clearing in the forest and saw that the Aucas were living there, Jim knew the time was coming close that he would meet the Aucas.

They needed a plan, and that's what they were working on in October of 1955. "Operation Auca" began.

They decided first to try to contact the Aucas from the air. They could use Nate Saint's plane and take gifts to the Aucas. Nate rigged a line to the plane that would let them lower a bucket and drop it within reach of the Aucas without having to land the plane. Their first gift was a small aluminum kettle with a lid. Inside it, the missionaries put some bright buttons and ribbons.

They did not see any Aucas that day, but they could see the clearing in the forest, and

THEY DECIDED TO CONTACT THE AUCAS BY AIR.

they left the kettle there. Later they saw that the kettle was gone; they knew the Aucas had found their gift.

The missionaries all had other work to do; they could not spend all their time looking for the Aucas, although they might have liked to do that. Instead, they decided to fly over the Auca territory once a week and leave a gift.

They chose a new spot for the second gift. The Aucas stayed hidden in the forest—except for one, a man. He peered up into the sky at the plane. Then he went and got two of his friends. Now Nate and Jim and Ed felt sure that the Aucas had picked up the first gift, and these men thought that the plane might leave something else. Their second gift was a machete, something very valuable to a tribe that lived apart from modern civilization.

The next week, Nate had a hard time

THEIR SECOND GIFT WAS A MACHETE.

regaining altitude after dropping the gift. He soon saw that the Aucas had taken hold of the line that the bucket hung from and did not want to let go.

Every week the Aucas got more curious about what the mysterious plane would bring. More and more of the tribespeople came out of hiding to see the plane.

Jim's turn to ride with Nate came during the fourth week of flights. Once they were in the air, he took out his phrase cards. Using a battery-powered loudspeaker, Jim shouted out in the Auca language, "I like you! I am your friend! You will be given a pot." Then he dropped the pot and waited for the Aucas to scramble over and get it.

The Aucas no longer were afraid; they were grateful for the gifts and started sending gifts back—a bird, a monkey, food.

"I LIKE YOU. I AM YOUR FRIEND."

A few weeks later, Jim had another chance to fly with Nate. This time he noticed that the Aucas had used the machetes to clear some of the forest, and now their houses were more visible. Jim got ready to drop another machete and a pair of pants. An old man stood beside one house and waved both his arms as if he wanted them to land the plane right there. For years, Jim had yearned to go to the Aucas. Nothing had made him forget about them. He had plenty of work to do at Shandia, teaching and preaching. And now he had a wife and a daughter. But still he wanted to go to the Aucas. He could hardly believe that he was coming close to his dream.

Jim, Ed, and Nate were encouraged by the response that their visits from the air were getting. Before long, they were talking about the next step—contact with the Aucas on the ground.

AN OLD MAN STOOD AND WAVED HIS ARMS.

Jim was especially eager to move ahead with their plan.

Ground contact could be very dangerous, they knew. They would not have the safety of an airplane, and they would have to be very careful about what they did. Jim started writing out plans, step-by-step.

Jim, Ed, and Nate were all planning to be part of Operation Auca. But they wanted to include some other people, too. Roger Youderian was a missionary who had worked with two tribes in Ecuador, and he was interested in Operation Auca. And Pete Fleming, Jim's partner in the early Shandia days, was interested. So the team would have five members.

Together the team had to decide their next step. Nate thought that they should continue with their flights and dropping gifts, perhaps doing it more often. Ed thought they should

THEY PLANNED "OPERATION AUCA."

concentrate on finding a place where they could clear an airstrip to land the plane. Jim wanted to do something soon. If they went into Auca territory with canoes, they would not have to wait to clear an airstrip. Pete was not sure the time was right; the Aucas were very dangerous, and the missionaries should move slowly. While they pondered what to do next, they continued their weekly flights.

By now, the Aucas had figured out that the plane came every seven days, and they stood in the clearings looking for the plane. Nate was confident enough to fly the plane closer to the ground now. He could look into the faces of the Aucas and see their friendly expressions. The Aucas were not afraid of the missionaries. Should the missionaries be afraid of the Aucas?

As they began to plan their next step, the

HE COULD SEE THE FACES OF THE AUCAS.

missionaries tried to think of everything that might happen. They could go in and set up a temporary camp along the river and wait for the Aucas to come to them. If they sensed any danger, they would leave immediately. They knew the Aucas could turn on them without warning, and they were experts with spears. What would the missionaries do then?

They decided to take guns with them—but only to frighten wild animals. They would not shoot at the Aucas. They would not use guns to save their lives. But then, no one thought that the Aucas were going to hurt them.

Everybody would have a job. Nate found a place on the beach where he thought he could land the plane, so they would not have to go by canoe. They called the place Palm Beach. Jim would be in charge of constructing a tree-house for the team, so they would be out of

NATE FOUND A PLACE TO LAND THE PLANE.

reach of animals at night. Roger made up the first-aid kit, and Ed collected items that they could trade with the Aucas. Pete would fly in and out of Palm Beach with Nate each day taking supplies.

They were ready.

ROGER MADE UP THE FIRST AID KIT.

NO ONE WANTED TO WAIT SEVERAL MONTHS.

8

They set the date for January 3, 1956. If they did not go then, they would have to wait until after the rainy season. The rainy season would last several months, and during that time it would be difficult to travel or to live for a few days on the beach without a real building to stay in. No one wanted to wait several more months, so the men made their plans to go to Palm Beach right after the holidays. At Christmastime, when several missionary families were together, they made their final decisions about what they would do to contact the Aucas on the ground.

Jim was not sure that Pete Fleming should go to Palm Beach. Pete was Jim's first partner, and Jim respected Pete. And Pete wanted to find the Aucas as much as anyone. But Jim thought Pete might be too valuable to risk, especially because he had learned Quichua. Jim was thinking about the work at Shandia and Puyupungu. If Pete joined the team and then something happened, all the men who could speak Quichua would be lost. This would be a major setback to the missionary work among the Quichuas.

Ed McCully jumped in, objecting to Jim's idea. Ed had a wife and two little boys, and his

ED MCCULLY OBJECTED TO JIM'S IDEA.

wife was pregnant with their third child. He told everyone that if he thought anything dangerous was going to happen to them, he would not be going. If Pete wanted to go, he should go. In the end, Nate said that he really needed Pete's help. Ed, Jim, and Roger would stay on the beach. Pete and Nate would fly in with supplies each morning, spend the day, then fly out before dark. Pete decided to go.

The men had decided what they were going to do. Their wives still had to decide how they felt about Operation Auca. Even though Ed had convinced the men that they had no reason to be afraid, the women knew that what their husbands were doing was risky. They had their own quiet conversations about what might happen.

The day came for Jim to fly from Shandia to Arajuno, the place that they were using as a

THE WOMEN DISCUSSED WHAT MIGHT HAPPEN.

base for Operation Auca. Elisabeth helped him pack his things, including items that might help entertain the Aucas and give the men time to show their friendship. Jim took a harmonica, a View-Master with pictures, and a yoyo, as well as some practical things, like a snakebite kit, a flashlight, and his Auca language cards. Today was the day he had been waiting for; he was going to the Aucas. He felt as ready as he could be, and he had no doubt that this was the right thing to do.

As Jim headed out of the house toward the plane, Elisabeth held her tongue. If Jim had any sense of danger, he did not show it, and she tried not to show how she felt. She wanted to say, "Do you realize you may never open that door again?" But she didn't. She simply walked out to the plane with him, where Jim kissed her good-bye as if he would be back in a few hours.

JIM GATHERED HIS SUPPLIES.

He hopped in next to the pilot and waved good-bye. Elisabeth stood on the lonely airstrip and watched the plane disappear from view as the sound of its engine grew faint.

That night, the five men gathered in Arajuno: Ed McCully, Nate Saint, Roger Youderian, Pete Fleming, and Jim Elliot. They had to get down to the details that would make their plan work. They stayed up late trying to think of everything that might happen so they could be ready for it. Every movement they would make the next day had to be planned out in detail. Nate would have to make several trips from Arajuno to Palm Beach. They made lists of all the equipment they would take with them on each trip and double-checked to make sure everything was working. Certain items would go in first so they could build a shelter. Less important items would follow on later

THEY DOUBLE CHECKED THEIR LIST.

trips. Nate could only fly during daylight hours, so they had to make sure they had everything they needed at Palm Beach before dark.

After hours of planning, the details were in place. They were as ready as they were ever going to be. No one slept much that night as they waited for the dawn.

In the morning, the plan called for Ed and Nate to make the first flight at eight o'clock. At the last minute, the plane had a problem with the brake fluid. Nate was an excellent mechanic as well as a pilot, so he fixed the problem, and they took off right on time. The sky was foggy that morning, which made it hard to spot the beach where they wanted to land. But just as they approached the beach, the fog thinned out, and they could see where they were going.

Nate flew over the beach one time to make

THE PLANE HAD A PROBLEM.

sure he knew where he wanted to land and looked for any objects that might damage the small plane. The beach seemed clear; it would be safe to land the plane. He set it down precisely between two trees and brought it to a halt.

From the air, Ed and Nate could see trees and other obstacles, but they could not be sure what the sand would be like. Now they found out that it was soft—too soft. As they came to a stop at the river's edge, they felt the plane sink into the sand. For a moment, their stomachs were in their throats. The plane could flip over and be ruined; they would be stranded on the beach. But the sand held. It was just firm enough to keep the plane from flipping over.

Ecstatic finally to be on Palm Beach, Nate and Ed jumped out, unloaded their equipment, and ran up and down the beach looking for things that might cause problems later.

ED AND NATE SEARCHED FOR POSSIBLE PROBLEMS.

After a few minutes of clearing the beach, it was time for Nate to take off again. He needed to be able to get the plane going at a fast speed on the ground before lifting into the air. But the sand was too soft; the plane's wheels would not move. Aware that precious minutes were ticking away, Ed and Nate leaned on the plane with all their weight and pushed it back, away from the water and into some bushes. The ground was firmer here, but Nate would not have as much room as he wanted for taking off. For a few stressful minutes, he did not know if he could take off at all. But his first try was successful, and he was on his way back to Arajuno.

Ed McCully was alone on the Auca beach, unarmed and exposed to threats from wild animals or unfriendly Aucas.

On the second flight, Nate took Roger and Jim to Palm Beach. Now there were three men

ED MCCULLY WAS ALONE ON THE BEACH.

on the beach. On the third trip, Nate took in the radio, some tools, and the basics Jim needed to start work on the treehouse. Jim organized the men as they worked, and that night they slept thirty-five feet off the ground, safe from whatever might prowl around the base of the tree.

Jim wrote a note to Elisabeth that night for Nate to take to her the next day. He wrote about the mosquitos and the beauty of the jungle. His words were hopeful; he was excited that perhaps the next day would be the day that they would reach the Aucas at last. Being on Palm Beach in close range of the Aucas was the dream he had been waiting for.

THEY SLEPT 35 FEET OFF THE GROUND.

NATE AND PETE FLEW OUT EVERY DAY.

9

The waiting began. The men were settled on the beach, Nate and Pete were flying in and out every day, and radio contact with Marj Saint at Shell Mera was clear. They were ready. But where were the Aucas? The men felt sure they were being watched, and the gifts they left on the beach were picked up during the dark nights, but they never actually saw any Aucas.

Once, just as they landed, Nate and Pete saw clear human footprints near the beach—and not just one or two. Not sure whether to believe the footprints were human, Jim Elliot ran downstream along the beach to inspect them close up. He found footprints of various sizes—proof that the Aucas had been nearby within the last few days.

They had to keep waiting. With their camp set up, they did not have much to do to pass the time. Jim read aloud from a novel, and they floated in the river water to try to get away from the heat and the bugs.

The third day on the beach began just as the first two. Pete and Nate flew in early in the morning to spend the day with the team on Palm Beach. The men took turns standing along the river and shouting Auca phrases into the jungle. If the Aucas were as near as the

JIM FOUND FOOT PRINTS.

missionaries thought, they could come out at any moment. Jim and the others used every friendly, encouraging phrase they had learned in the Auca language.

Suddenly, a male voice answered one of their calls! Although they had been hoping for an answer, they were still surprised when it came. Three Aucas stepped out of the trees and into clear view, a young man and two women. They wore no clothes, but they had strings tied around their waists, wrists, and legs. They also had wooden plugs stuck through holes in their earlobes.

The five missionaries jumped to their feet, instantly alert. They called out, "Puinani! Welcome!" The Aucas stood on the opposite side of the river, examining the strange out-siders, who looked so odd, yet spoke familiar words.

THREE AUCAS STEPPED OUT OF THE TREES.

The Auca man started to talk, but the missionaries could not understand him. They did not know very many words, and he was talking too fast. They had been practicing speaking Auca phrases, but that was not the same as hearing an Auca speak the language. So the missionaries tried "talking" without words; they started watching what the man did with his hands instead of just listening to his voice.

Suddenly, Jim pulled off his shirt and pants and plunged into the water. He understood what they wanted! They wanted someone to help them across the river, and he was going to do it. He was not going to miss this chance to get close to the Aucas, not after waiting so long to get to this point.

The other missionaries called out to Jim to be careful. If he got into trouble in the middle of the river, they would not be able to help him.

SUDDENLY JIM TOOK OFF HIS SHIRT.

And once he got to the other side, the Aucas might decide to attack, and there would be no one to protect him. For a fraction of a second, Jim slowed down and glanced over his shoulder at his friends. Then he kept going. He did not think he would be attacked. It seemed to him that the three Aucas wanted to be friends. All he had to do was convince them that he wanted to be friends, too.

Once Jim was on the way, one of the women cautiously stepped off a log on the other side and into the water, followed by the man and the other woman. Jim offered his hand, and the young woman took it. He led them safely across the river. His mind pounded with the thought that he was actually touching an Auca! He had spoken Auca words and they had understood him. He was sure they were responding to his friendship.

JIM OFFERED HIS HAND.

Once back on the other side, Jim scrambled to get out his language cards. He wanted to tell the Aucas that they had nothing to be afraid of. He managed to get this idea across, and the Aucas relaxed. All three of them started talking. They did not seem to notice that the missionaries did not understand them.

The missionaries had come prepared with gifts—knives, machetes, a model airplane. One of the women was fascinated by a copy of a magazine. They also got out their cameras and starting snapping pictures. The Aucas did not seem to mind, although they did not know what a camera was.

The three Indians were curious and friendly. The missionaries gave them names. The man was George, and the younger woman was Delilah. And they kept talking with their hands.

Delilah walked over to the plane and started

THEY GOT OUT THEIR CAMERAS.

to inspect it. She had never seen a plane close up. She rubbed herself against it, then stretched her arms out to the side to playfully swoop as she had seen it do.

George was soon beside her. But he had not come across the river just to look and touch. He had bigger plans. George pointed and gestured until the missionaries realized that he wanted a ride in the plane. He showed them how he would call out to the people below as he had seen the missionaries do.

Jim and the others looked at each other. They had not expected this, and they were not sure what to do. They quickly decided to let him fly. George was no danger to them. Why shouldn't they do what he asked. George could help their work a lot and help them to meet the leaders of his tribe. Besides, George was ready to go, and it did not look like he would

HE WANTED TO RIDE IN THE PLANE.

change his mind.

Finally, Nate climbed in beside George and started the engine.

George paid no attention to Nate. Instead, he leaned out the opening next to him to see where he had come from. He saw his village below and yelled and waved to his people. He was pleased with his achievement. Who else in his tribe could claim such an experience?

The missionaries had thought out how they would communicate their needs to the Aucas. Once George was back on the ground, they gathered around him. Someone stuck sticks in the sand to represent trees, then pulled out a small model of the plane. They showed how the plane could not land on the ground because of too many trees. Then they took away some of the sticks and showed how the plane could land easily in a clear space. The look in

THEY SHOWED HOW THE PLANE COULD LAND.

George's eyes told them that he understood: the missionaries could not fly to his village because of the trees. But if the Aucas would take out some of the trees, then the plane could come to his people.

This kind of sign language went on all afternoon as the Aucas tried out all the little gadgets the missionaries had with them—rubberbands, balloons, yoyos. The men even fixed lemonade and hamburgers for their guests. Jim felt that they were really making contact. He hoped that George might invite them to his village. But so far George did not seem interested in that.

Nate and Pete had to leave before dark, so they gathered up all the film everyone had used and the notes they had taken. They wanted to be sure these things got to a safe place. Before climbing up into their treehouse, Jim, Ed, and Roger

THE MEN FIXED LEMONADE AND BURGERS.

offered their kitchen shack to the Aucas for shelter. Delilah was not interested and wandered into the forest. After a few minutes, George followed her. The older woman stayed on the beach, tending a fire most of the night. But in the morning she was gone. A ring of smoldering coals was the only evidence of her presence.

And the waiting began again. Jim and the rest of the team had no way to know if George would come back or if others from the village would come. Their excitement swelled as they thought about reaching a tribe deep in the Ecuador jungle, people who had never seen a church, never read a book, never sung a hymn, never heard a missionary preach. But they had to keep waiting. Hour after hour they waited on the beach, grasping at activities to keep themselves busy.

In the middle of that long, quiet day, Jim

A RING OF COALS SMOLDERED.

grew restless and impatient. "I give them five minutes," he said to the others. "If they don't show up, I'm going over." His common sense returned, though, and he did not go. It was so hard to wait and not be able to do anything more to reach his goal.

Finally, two days after George and the woman had visited, Nate got restless and took the plane up during the day to check around. He flew over the village. There were only a few women and children walking around the clearing. Where were the men? A moment later, he saw them. They were marching as a group toward the beach. Swiftly, he turned the plane around and returned the beach. He jumped out, shouting, "This is it, guys! They're on the way!" The others put down their books and got ready to meet an official welcoming committee of Aucas.

THE MEN MARCHED TOWARD THE BEACH.

Nate got on the radio to communicate with his wife. It was 12:30. Excitedly, he told Marj about the approaching men and promised to radio again at 4:30 with news of the meeting.

Standing on the beach waiting for the Auca men to arrive, Jim Elliot had no regrets about being the first one to wade into the river two days earlier. He knew that years of patient preparation were about to be rewarded. He had waited a long time for this day.

HE HAD WAITED A LONG TIME FOR THIS DAY.

BUT THE RADIO WAS SILENT.

10

Promptly at 4:30, Marj Saint was at the radio waiting for contact from her husband. Pete Fleming's wife, Olive, had been ill and was recuperating at Shell Mera. Together, they huddled at the radio waiting for the familiar crackle that would mean their husbands were at the other end. But the radio was silent. Marj checked her watch to make sure she had the time right. She did. They watched the clock as 4:30 passed, then 4:45, then 5:00.

Nate Saint was a stickler about communication. To him, staying in radio contact frequently and regularly was a rule that should never be broken. He always let Marj know where he was and what his condition was. He never, ever forgot. So why did he not call this time?

Marj and Olive speculated that perhaps the radio on the beach had broken down since Nate's last call. But Marj was not satisfied with that explanation. The men had planned for the possibility that the radio might fail; there were two radios on the beach. If one was not working, Nate would use the other one. That was no explanation. Silence could not be good news.

Soon it was too dark to expect that Nate and Pete could fly back that night as they had been

SILENCE COULD NOT BE GOOD NEWS.

doing. Marj turned off the radio.

Marj and Olive passed the evening with routine activities and did not alarm any of the other missionary wives or the guests at Shell Mera. But they did not sleep much. Finally, the long night passed. In the morning, Marj and Olive came face to face with the reality that they had feared during the dark hours of lying awake. There was still no word from Nate.

Johnny Keenan, another missionary pilot, took a plane up and flew over the area where Operation Auca was based. Within a few minutes, he was on the radio with Marj—with bad news. He had spotted Nate's plane, stripped of all its yellow fabric and not in any condition to be flown. He saw no sign of the five men, but the damage to the plane—along with Nate's silence—clearly meant something was wrong.

Now Marj called the other wives. Barbara

HE SPOTTED NATE'S PLANE—STRIPPED.

Youderian and Marilou McCully came in from Arajuno. Elisabeth Elliot arrived from Shandia, along with Rachel Saint, Nate's sister. They gathered in Marj's spacious, comfortable home, fearful of what had brought them together. Obviously, the men had fallen into danger—but just what had happened? Nearly everyone was hopeful that at least some of the men had survived and would be able to tell them the whole story. Marilou McCully was so convinced of this that she did not stay at Shell Mera with the others; she went back to her house at Arajuno. Since her house was the closest to where the men had gone, they would go there first when they came out of Auca territory. She wanted to be home when they arrived.

Another day passed. By now, word had gone out around the world that the five missionaries were missing.

WHAT HAD HAPPENED?

On the third day, Johnny Keenan flew over the river again. This time he spotted a body floating in the river. From the air, it was hard to tell who it was, and Johnny did not dare try to land and retrieve the body. But it meant that at least one of the men had not survived. The women, holding their small children in their arms, all looked at each other, knowing that at least one of them was now a widow. Fear for the well-being of all their husbands multiplied.

Three days of silence dimmed the hopes that anyone had survived. Marilou McCully had waited patiently at Arajuno, but no one had come.

On the fourth day, the Air Force Rescue Operation joined the search that a network of missionaries and Quichuas had started. Now searchers could cover more territory in a less amount of time. The Air Force also could give

HE SAW A BODY FLOATING IN THE RIVER.

protection to the searchers on the ground, in case someone was still alive.

The wives kept waiting, taking care of their young children and passing one hour at a time.

Finally, someone sent for Marilou McCully to come back to Shell Mera. The women braced themselves for the news that the searchers brought.

Four bodies had been spotted from the air, and the Quichuas on the ground had found the fifth. The bodies had not been identified, but there were five. No one had survived. There was no information on what had happened, and no way to find out what had provoked the attack when every sign was that the Aucas were responding to the missionaries' friendship.

The Aucas themselves retreated into the jungle, once again beyond reach.

THERE WERE FIVE BODIES.

OLIVE AND MARILOU SET UP SCHOOL.

11

With their husbands gone, each of the women had to decide whether they would stay in Ecuador or return to the United States. Marilou McCully decided to return to the States for the birth of her third son. Later, she returned to set up a home for missionary children who attended school in Quito. Olive Fleming helped Marilou set up the school and then returned to the States permanently. Barbara Youderian returned to work with the Jivaros, the tribe she and Roger had worked with before. Marj Saint took up a new job in Quito. Elisabeth Elliot returned to Shandia, where she continued working with Rachel Saint.

Rachel was studying the Auca language with Dayuma, the young woman who had helped Jim Elliot learn key phrases of friendship. Shortly after the killings at Palm Beach, Rachel Saint showed Dayuma photographs of "George" and "Delilah" and the other woman. The men had taken a camera to the beach and used it before their deaths. Now Dayuma got excited. She recognized the older woman as her own aunt and the younger woman as her cousin. Dayuma had left the Aucas because of a brutal family feud. She had never been sure whether any of her family was still alive.

DAYUMA SAW PHOTOS OF GEORGE AND DELILAH.

Knowing that her aunt and cousin were alive gave her hope that others in her family had survived. This information made her think that perhaps she could go back to her own people after years of living among the Quichuas.

Because of those photos, Dayuma became a bridge between outsiders and her own people. Elisabeth and Rachel had already decided to take up where the men left off and try to reach the Aucas. Without Dayuma, it might have been impossible for the missionaries to continue any contact with the tribe. Friendship did not happen right away, but eventually, the Aucas started responding to the missionaries again.

Elisabeth and Jim Elliot had talked about going to live among the Aucas as a family someday, and Elisabeth was still willing to do this. She took her young daughter, Valerie, and

DAYUMA HELPED OTHER MISSIONARIES SEE THE AUCAS.

moved to the Auca village. Rachel Saint, Nate's sister, went with her. Once they were settled there, they could do more intensive language study and eventually present Christianity to the Aucas. Dayuma continued to help them, and she herself became a Christian. While she lived among the tribe, Elisabeth collected information about that day on Palm Beach, trying to find out just what happened to Jim and the others—and why.

Elisabeth left the Auca work after a few years and returned to live in the United States. Rachel Saint stayed on with the Aucas for many years. Eventually, many of the Aucas became Christians. Rachel nurtured the church, which was led by some of the same men who had killed her brother and the others. The tribe was now known as the Waorani, which was their own name for themselves. "Auca" was a

RACHEL HELPED THE AUCA CHURCH GROW.

Quichua word that meant savagery. Now that they were Christians, the tribe did not want the world to know them by their old reputation. Rachel and other missionaries worked for many years to put the Waorani language in a written form—just as Jim Elliot had wanted to do. They looked forward to having the Bible in Waorani.

More than thirty years after the killings, Olive Fleming returned to the scene. She had remarried about two years after Pete's death and now traveled to Ecuador with her husband and the youngest of their three children. Unlike thirty-three years earlier, it was now perfectly safe for Olive and her family to visit Palm Beach.

Except for one flight over the watery grave with the other widows, Olive had never seen Palm Beach. Now she sat where the men had

IT WAS NOW SAFE TO VISIT PALM BEACH.

built their shelter, although the beach had changed over the years. Even the tree that had once held the treehouse thirty-five feet off the ground had been wrenched out of the ground by high water.

One of the Waorani women, Dawa, started speaking. Rachel Saint translated for Olive and the others.

Dawa told about that day long ago. She had seen what happened from a hiding place in the forest. The missionaries had not used their guns to defend themselves. They had decided before they ever went to Palm Beach that they would not fire on the Aucas, and when the time came, they stood by their decision. They fired into the air, trying to frighten their attackers, but they let the Waorani kill them.

Rachel Saint had heard this story before. But Dawa went on with something Rachel had never heard before. Dawa told how, on the day that

THEY FIRED INTO THE AIR.

George and the others had visited the beach, one of the men had taken something out of his pocket to show them. In 1956, the Aucas did not wear clothing and did not understand what a pocket was. It seemed to them that the man was taking something out of his body. What he took out was a photograph of Dayuma. The missionaries had carried the photo in hope that the Aucas would recognize Dayuma and know that she was still alive. But just as they did not understand pockets, the Aucas did not understand photography. They did recognize Dayuma, but what had happened to her? What had the strangers done to Dayuma to make her flat and small? How could Dayuma come out of the man's body? How had she gotten in there? The obvious conclusion was that the man had eaten Dayuma.

When the three visitors told this story to the

THE MISSIONARIES SHOWED DAYUMA'S PHOTO.

rest of the tribe, fear spread that the missionaries wanted to eat the whole group.

And so the Aucas killed the missionaries.

Kimo, a Waorani Christian leader, now joined Dawa's story. He and Dawa, with the others hiding in the jungle during the attack, had looked over the top of the trees and seen what looked like "a hundred flashlights." At the time they did not understand what they were seeing. Later, when they had become Christians, they knew they had seen angels and heard them singing. Dawa told Rachel that it was the vision on the beach that first persuaded her to believe in God, and Dawa had become the first Christian in the tribe five years later.

Rachel Saint was as surprised by this information as Olive Fleming Liefeld was. She had lived among these people a long time. Why had she not heard this story before? No one can say

THEY SAW ANGELS AND HEARD THEM SING.

why Dawa did not tell her story sooner.

Jim Elliot, along with Pete, Ed, Roger, and Nate, gave his life trying to reach the Aucas. At the time, it might have seemed that they failed. But thirty-three years later, a once savage tribe was living peacefully with its neighbors and teaching the Christian faith. According to Dawa and Kimo, it all started with a vision on the beach when the men were killed.

Three years after Olive's visit to Palm Beach, and thirty-six years after the deaths of the men, the Waoranis celebrated having the entire New Testament in their own language—the work Jim Elliot had hoped to do. Although his part in the dream was not what he thought it would be, Jim Elliot's dream of a lifetime had been fulfilled.

JIM ELLIOT'S DREAM HAD BEEN FULFILLED.

Key Dates
in the Life of Jim Elliot

October 1927
    Jim Elliot is born in Oregon
September 1945
    Jim enters Wheaton College in Wheaton,
    Illinois
May 1948
    Jim and Elisabeth realize they love each
    other
June 1948
    Elisabeth graduates from college and leaves
    Wheaton
Spring 1949
    Jim challenges Ed McCully to be a
    missionary

June 1949
    Jim graduates from Wheaton and returns to
    Portland, Oregon
Summer 1950
    Jim attends linguistic training in Oklahoma;
    Bill Cathers and David Howard get
    married; Jim commits to going to Ecuador
Fall 1950
    Ed McCully decides to leave law school
    and consider missionary work
January 1951
    Jim begins ministry in Chester, Illinois,
    with Ed McCully
June 1951
    Ed McCully gets married; Jim returns to
    Oregon
February 1952
    Jim and Pete Fleming arrive in Ecuador

April 1952

Elisabeth arrives in Ecuador

August 1952

Jim and Pete finish language study and go to the Shandia mission station

December 1952

Ed and Marilou McCully arrive in Ecuador

July 1953

Flood at Shandia destroys a year's work

October 1953

Jim and Elisabeth get married in Quito; move to Puyupungu to establish new station

June 1954

Jim and Elisabeth move to Shandia

February 1955

Jim and Elisabeth's daughter, Valerie, is born at Shell Mera

September 1955
    Nate Saint and Ed McCully see the Aucas
    for the first time
October 1955
    Search for Aucas begins in earnest; first gift
    drop made
December 1955
    Plans finalized for ground contact with
    Aucas
January 3, 1956
    The missionaries land on Palm Beach and
    set up camp
January 6, 1956
    George, Delilah, and another woman come
    to the beach
January 8, 1956
    Last radio contact with Marj Saint at Shell
    Mera

AWESOME BOOKS FOR KIDS!

The Young Reader's Christian Library
Action, Adventure, and Fun Reading!

This series for young readers ages 8 to 12 is action-packed, fast-paced, and Christ-centered! With exciting illustrations on every other page following the text, kids won't be able to put these books down! Over 100 illustrations per book. All books are paperbound. The unique size (4 ⅛" x 5 ⅜") makes these books easy to take anywhere!

A Great Selection to Satisfy All Kids!

Abraham Lincoln	Heidi	Pollyanna
Ben-Hur	Hudson Taylor	Prudence of Plymouth
Billy Graham	In His Steps	Plantation
Billy Sunday	Jesus	Robinson Crusoe
Christopher Columbus	Joseph	Roger Williams
Corrie ten Boom	Lydia	Ruth
David Brainerd	Miriam	Samuel Morris
David Livingstone	Moses	The Swiss Family
Deborah	Paul	Robinson
Elijah	Peter	Taming the Land
Esther	The Pilgrim's Progress	Thunder in the Valley
Florence Nightingale	Pocahontas	Wagons West

Available wherever books are sold.
Or order from: Barbour Publishing, Inc., P.O. Box 719
Uhrichsville, Ohio 44683
http://www.barbourbooks.com